OMELETTES, SOUFFLÉS & FRITTATAS

OMELETTES, SOUFFLÉS & FRITTATAS

lou seibert pappas

PHOTOGRAPHS BY
e. j. armstrong

CHRONICLE BOOKS
SAN FRANCISCO

Text copyright © 1999 by LOU SEIBERT PAPPAS.
Photographs copyright © 1999 by E. J. ARMSTRONG.
Library of Congress Cataloging-in-Publication Data:
Pappas, Lou Seibert.
        Omelettes, soufflés, and frittatas / by Lou Seibert Pappas.
                p.   cm.
        Includes index.
        ISBN 0-8118-2120-X (PB)
        1. Omelettes.   2. Soufflés.   I. Title
    TX745.P37   1999
    641.6'75–dc21   98-30315
                            CIP

Printed in Hong Kong

Prop styling by PATTY WHITMAN
Food styling by PATTY WHITMAN
Designed and typeset by ANNE GALPERIN

Distributed in Canada by
Raincoast Books
8680 Cambie Street
Vancouver, British Columbia V6P 6M9

10 9 8 7 6 5 4 3 2

Chronicle Books
85 Second Street
San Francisco, California 94105

www.chroniclebooks.com

CONTENTS

INTRODUCTION

tthe egg is a marvel of package design: exquisitely simple, yet enormously complex. Economical, versatile, and naturally high in nutrition, its potential in the kitchen is boundless.

Omelettes, frittatas, and soufflés are the good cook's friend: fast and easy to whip up at a moment's notice. Yet they are surrounded with an aura of mystique, as if they were creations produced by a genie in the kitchen. Set forth a soufflé to guests, and they go into raptures. But these ethereal creations are easy to master, bringing surprise and delight to the table.

Omelettes have been known in France for centuries and in England since about 1600. The French word *omelette* is said to derive from the Latin *lamella,* meaning "thin plate," according to Harold McGee in his excellent volume *On Food and Cooking.* Today, the word *omelette* is often used loosely to cover a range of beaten-egg dishes cooked in a pan.

Stove-top omelettes are last-minute affairs to be turned out on a whim. They take less than a minute to prepare from pan to plate. And with nonstick pans they can be prepared with very little or no butter. Oven omelettes can be assembled in advance, ready for a special brunch or weekend breakfast. A frittata is an omelette that is cooked like a pancake and left unfolded. It is often served at room temperature, cut into wedges or squares, as an appetizer or entrée. The filling can vary, depending on the bounty of the larder and the inspiration of the cook.

The word *soufflé* stems from the French verb *souffler,* meaning "to blow, breathe, or whisper," suggesting the fragility of these ethereal creations. Soufflés generally have a sauce base into which may be incorporated cheese, cooked or puréed vegetables, meats, seafood, or fruit. Once assembled, some soufflés can be prepared an hour or two or even a day ahead and refrigerated, then popped into a hot oven and baked to present hot and puffy at the table. Most cooks are unaware of this unique bonus feature, and think of soufflés as strictly last-minute affairs.

Soufflé omelettes are a combination of both dishes, made with separated eggs cooked in a skillet, then baked. Often they are faster to prepare than a traditional soufflé, as they lack a sauce base. The yolks and whites are beaten separately so the omelette puffs nicely, and they may incorporate a sauce or fruit for extra flavor. They are baked on top of the stove to set the underside before a final oven finish to puff and brown.

I hope you will enjoy the egg recipes in this book for both impromptu meals and party fare.

THE EGG ITSELF

An egg is considered one of nature's most nearly perfect foods, and its nutritive value is high. One large egg (about 2 ounces) contains 75 calories, 6 grams of protein, and about 5 grams of fat. Of this, about 1.5 grams is saturated, and the majority is mainly heart-healthy unsaturated fatty acids. Each egg contains varying amounts of 13 vitamins, in particular A and D, and is especially high in iron and calcium.

The yolk makes up just over one-third of an egg, and provides three-fourths of the calories; all of the fat and vitamins A, D, and E; most of the choline, phosphorous, iron, and calcium; and almost half of the protein and riboflavin. The white has more than half the total protein and riboflavin.

Cholesterol is part of every human cell and is essential to the body, yet eggs have been shunned because of their relatively high cholesterol. The latest data indicates that eggs contain less dietary cholesterol than previously thought. A large egg averages 213 milligrams cholesterol, not the 274 milligrams listed in most references.

The color of the eggshell does not affect the nutritional value of the egg. The breed of the hen determines the color of the shell, and the yolk color depends on the diet of the hen.

The occasional blood spot in an egg is caused by the rupture of a blood vessel on the yolk surface during formation of the egg. It is both chemically and nutritionally fit to eat, but can be removed with the tip of a knife.

Eggs are graded according to quality and freshness. Grade AA, the highest-quality table egg, is the most desirable grade for eating. The recipes in this book are based on large eggs, the accepted size for all recipes in most cookbooks.

FRESHNESS & STORAGE To preserve freshness, store eggs in the refrigerator in the carton just as they are packed: blunt end up, which keeps the yolk centered. Do not place eggs near any strong-flavored foods, since their shells are porous. Do not leave eggs out at room temperature. They will age more in one day at room temperature than they will in one week in the refrigerator, and room temperature is an ideal temperature for bacterial growth.

Avoid using any eggs that are cracked, chipped, or broken when purchased, as they could be contaminated with salmonella bacteria.

As an egg ages, the white becomes thinner and the yolk becomes flatter. The egg also becomes more alkaline and develops hydrogen sulfide, a compound of disagreeable odor that smells like some mineral waters. Overly long cooking or high temperature encourages the development of this odor and flavor, even in a freshly laid egg.

Egg whites may be stored in a covered jar in the refrigerator for up to 4 days. They may also be frozen; thaw them in the refrigerator and use them exactly as you would fresh egg whites. Egg yolks will also freeze, but they do not soften completely when thawed. Store raw egg yolks in a container and cover them with a thin layer of cold water, then refrigerate and use within 1 to 2 days.

The different egg proteins coagulate at different temperatures, producing thickening. When the egg coagulates, it first forms a clot, like a lacy network. If overheating occurs, the network contracts, forcing out the liquid. This is why it is so important not to overcook egg dishes.

savory OMELETTES

SAVORY OMELETTES

the traditional French-style omelette is tender and firm outside and softer within. It is cooked over medium-high heat into a thin sheet, filled with one of a wide variety of fillings, then rolled or folded. Because of the concern of salmonella, it is wise to cook it thoroughly. The Spanish-style omelette is open-faced and often served cut in wedges as a tapa or appetizer. Other flat, frittata-style omelettes are included here as well.

The keys to making a good omelette are a good, medium-hot nonstick or well-seasoned pan and deft, quick skill. The classic French omelette pan has shallow sloping sides, a flat bottom, and a long handle. An individual omelette is best made with no more than 2 to 3 eggs in a 7- to 8-inch omelette pan or skillet. (A larger amount is difficult to roll and turn out of the pan. Instead, it may be served flat; slide it from the pan and cut in wedges.) Working swiftly, it is easy to cook an omelette in 30 seconds or less, so a succession of individual omelettes can be prepared easily. Serve each as soon as possible.

Beat the eggs just until blended and season with salt and pepper. Do not overbeat, as the eggs will develop less volume and taste "thin." Have the filling ready. Heat the skillet until hot over medium-high heat, add the butter, and when it stops foaming, quickly pour in the eggs. Tilt the pan and, using a spatula, lift the edge of the eggs to let the liquid part flow underneath, simultaneously shaking and tilting the pan to help it flow. (With a nonstick skillet, a spatula is unnecessary, as shaking the pan does the job.) In less than 20 to 30 seconds, when the omelette is set but still moist, spread the filling across the center and tilt the pan or use a spatula to help roll one-third of the omelette over onto itself. Turn out onto a warm plate, making another fold.

classic omelette in variation

THIS BASIC OMELETTE CAN BE FILLED IN COUNTLESS WAYS (SEE PAGE 16) FOR A LAST-MINUTE ENTRÉE AT ANY TIME OF DAY. GIVE THE PAN A GOOD TILT AS YOU POUR IN THE EGGS SO THEY FLOW EVENLY.

2 eggs

⅛ teaspoon salt

Freshly ground pepper to taste

1 teaspoon unsalted butter

In a small bowl, whisk the eggs, salt, and pepper together just until blended. Heat a 7-inch skillet over medium-high heat, add the butter, and when it stops foaming, tilt the pan to coat evenly. Add the eggs all at once. Shake the pan, slip a thin spatula under the eggs just as soon as they are set, and lift the eggs, tilting the pan to let the uncooked portion flow underneath. Fill, if desired, then roll over one-third of the omelette and tilt it onto a warm plate, making another fold.

Makes 1 serving

fillings

shredded Monterey Jack cheese and chopped green chilies

mixed minced fresh herbs such as tarragon, flat-leaf parsley, chives, basil, and marjoram

feta cheese and minced fresh dill

goat cheese and minced fresh chives or tarragon

caviar, sour cream, and chopped red onion or minced fresh chives

smoked salmon, sour cream, and minced fresh chives or chopped green onions

sautéed white or brown mushrooms, shallots, and goat cheese

crabmeat, bay scallops, or bay shrimp heated in butter, and minced fresh dill, cilantro, or chives

shredded Gruyère cheese and minced fresh chives

cooked asparagus tips, broccoli florets, or artichoke hearts, and Parmesan cheese

sautéed chopped spinach and chopped green onions

sliced avocado, mango chutney, and shredded Jarlsberg or Monterey Jack cheese

sautéed chopped red and yellow bell peppers, red onions, and minced fresh basil

ratatouille, shredded Gruyère, and minced fresh basil

bacon, leek & hazelnut gruyère omelette

FOR A SPUR-OF-THE-MOMENT SUNDAY LUNCH OR SUPPER DISH, THIS FESTIVE OPEN-FACE OMELETTE CAN BE PUT
TOGETHER SWIFTLY WITH INGREDIENTS GENERALLY ON HAND.

4 slices bacon, diced

⅓ cup skinned hazelnuts, coarsely
chopped

1 leek (white part only) or small
onion, finely chopped

6 eggs

Salt and freshly ground pepper to
taste

2 tablespoons butter

2 tablespoons minced fresh
flat-leaf parsley

¾ cup (3 ounces) shredded
Gruyère or Jarlsberg cheese

¼ cup plain yogurt

¼ cup sour cream

In an 8-inch omelette pan or skillet, cook the bacon over medium heat until crisp and browned. Transfer the bacon to paper towels to drain. Drain off all but 2 tablespoons of the drippings. Add the nuts to the pan and sauté until browned; remove from the pan. Sauté the leek or onion in the reserved drippings until soft, about 5 minutes; set aside.

Preheat the broiler. In a medium bowl, beat the eggs with the salt and pepper just until blended. In a 10-inch skillet over medium heat, melt the butter. Pour the eggs into the pan and sprinkle with the leek or onion, bacon, and parsley. Reduce the heat to low and cook, lifting the eggs with a spatula as they set and allowing the uncooked portion to flow under-neath. When the top of the omelette is almost set, sprinkle with the cheese and place under the broiler to heat through. Mix the yogurt and sour cream together and spoon into the center. Ring with the sautéed nuts. Cut into wedges to serve.

Makes 4 to 6 servings

jarlsberg oven omelette

A FAVORITE IN MY HOME FOR CHRISTMAS-MORNING BRUNCH, THIS FAST-TO-ASSEMBLE OVEN OMELETTE IS LACED WITH MELTED CHEESE AND RIBBONS OF PROSCIUTTO. IT CAN BE ASSEMBLED IN ADVANCE. WITH FRESH-BAKED PANETTONE AND A PLATTER OF FRESH FRUIT—SLICED ORANGES, BANANAS, KIWIFRUIT, AND STRAWBERRIES—IT MAKES A FESTIVE HOLIDAY MEAL.

8 eggs

1 cup milk

½ teaspoon salt

⅛ teaspoon ground white pepper

⅛ teaspoon ground nutmeg

2 ounces thinly sliced prosciutto or cooked ham, cut into strips

2½ cups (10 ounces) shredded Jarlsberg, Gruyère, or Samsoe cheese

1 tablespoon butter, melted

Preheat the oven to 350°F. Butter a 6-cup baking dish about 10½ inches in diameter.

In a large bowl, beat the eggs with a whisk just until blended. Mix in the milk, salt, pepper, nutmeg, prosciutto or ham, and cheese. Pour into the prepared dish. Drizzle the top with melted butter. Bake in the oven for 30 to 35 minutes, or until set and lightly browned.

Makes 6 to 8 servings

spanish omelette

THIS POPULAR SPANISH TAPA, OR APPETIZER, IS GOOD WITH A RIOJA WINE OR COCKTAILS. IT ALSO MAKES A LIGHT ENTRÉE FOR LUNCH OR SUPPER, ACCOMPANIED WITH CRUSTY BREAD AND A CAESAR SALAD.

3 tablespoons extra-virgin olive oil

⅓ cup diced ham

1 onion, finely chopped

1 red bell pepper, seeded, deribbed, and finely chopped

1 small Japanese eggplant, peeled and finely chopped

1 small zucchini, finely chopped

2 tomatoes, peeled, seeded, and finely chopped

6 eggs

Salt and freshly ground pepper to taste

2 tablespoons minced fresh basil

Preheat the broiler. In a 10-inch skillet over medium heat, heat the oil and sauté the ham, onion, and pepper until soft, about 5 minutes. Add the eggplant and zucchini and sauté until the vegetables are tender, about 5 minutes. Increase the heat to medium-high, add the tomatoes, and cook until the juices evaporate. Beat the eggs with salt and pepper and pour over the vegetables. Reduce the heat to low and cook until the underside is lightly browned.

Place under the broiler to brown the top side. Or, turn the omelette over by inverting it on a plate and sliding it back into the pan; cook until set. Sprinkle with the basil. Serve hot or at room temperature, cut into wedges.

Makes 8 to 10 appetizer servings
or 4 entrée servings

persian vegetable omelette

TOASTED PISTACHIOS ARE A CRUNCHY DELIGHT IN THIS VERDANT OVEN OMELETTE. THIS IS IDEAL FOR A SUMMER PICNIC OR GARDEN PARTY, ACCOMPANIED WITH SKEWERED SHRIMP OR GRILLED CHICKEN.

2 tablespoons olive oil

1 large bunch green onions, white and green parts, chopped

1 bunch spinach, stemmed and chopped

1⅓ cups chopped Swiss chard leaves (no stems) or iceberg lettuce

1 bunch fresh flat-leaf parsley, stemmed and minced

2 garlic cloves, minced

5 eggs

Salt and freshly ground pepper to taste

¼ cup pistachios or walnuts, toasted and chopped

6 cherry tomatoes, hulled and halved

3 tablespoons grated dry Monterey Jack or Romano cheese

Plain yogurt for serving (optional)

Preheat the oven to 350°F. Grease a 9-inch pie pan.

In a large skillet over medium-high heat, heat the oil and sauté the onions until soft, 2 to 3 minutes. Add the spinach, chard or lettuce, parsley, and garlic. Cook, stirring, for 2 to 3 minutes. Set aside.

In a large bowl, beat the eggs just until blended. Mix in the salt, pepper, sautéed vegetables, and half the nuts. Spoon into the prepared pan. Arrange the tomatoes, cut-side down, over the top. Sprinkle with the remaining nuts and the cheese.

Bake in the oven for 25 minutes, or until set. Let cool slightly and cut into wedges. Serve hot or at room temperature, with yogurt, if desired.

Makes 6 servings

smoked salmon & caramelized onion omelette

THIS IS A SAVORY VARIATION OF THE JEWISH SUNDAY BREAKFAST TREAT OF SCRAMBLED EGGS, CARAMELIZED ONIONS, AND SMOKED SALMON ON BAGELS. CANTALOUPE AND HONEYDEW MELON WEDGES MAKE A REFRESHING PARTNER.

4 eggs

Salt and freshly ground pepper to taste

1 tablespoon extra-virgin olive oil

1 large white onion, chopped

1 tablespoon unsalted butter

2 ounces smoked salmon, finely diced

2 tablespoons sour cream

Minced fresh chives for garnish

Toasted bagels for serving

In a medium bowl, beat the eggs with the salt and pepper just until blended. In a 9-inch skillet over medium heat, heat the oil and sauté the onion, stirring frequently, until soft and caramelized, 10 to 12 minutes. Turn out of the pan. In the same skillet, melt the butter over medium heat. Pour the eggs into the pan and cook, lifting from the edge to let the runny portion flow underneath; when almost set, scatter the onion and salmon over.

Roll over one-third of the omelette and tilt it onto a warm plate, making another fold. Spoon the sour cream over the top and sprinkle with the chives. Serve immediately, with warm bagels.

Makes 2 servings

german bacon & potato omelette

IF YOU HAVE LEFTOVER BOILED POTATOES, INCORPORATE THEM IN THIS HEARTY GERMAN OMELETTE FOR A TASTY
ENTRÉE FOR BRUNCH, LUNCH, OR SUPPER. BLACK RYE BREAD AND COLESLAW ARE GOOD ACCOMPANIMENTS.

2   unpeeled Yukon Gold potatoes

4   eggs

1   tablespoon sour cream

    Salt and freshly ground pepper
      to taste

6   slices bacon, diced

1   small onion, chopped

2   tablespoons minced fresh
      flat-leaf parsley

2   tablespoons minced fresh chives

Cook the potatoes in salted boiling water until barely tender, about 15 minutes. Drain, peel, and slice about ¼ inch thick.

Preheat the broiler. Meanwhile, in a medium bowl, beat the eggs just until blended. Mix in the sour cream, salt, and pepper. In a 10-inch skillet, sauté the bacon over medium heat until crisp and transfer to paper towels to drain. Pour off all but 2 tablespoons of the drippings and sauté the onion and potatoes until glazed.

Pour the eggs over the potato mixture and sprinkle with the bacon. Reduce the heat to low and cook until the eggs are set, shaking the pan to prevent them from sticking. Place under the broiler to heat through. Sprinkle with the parsley and chives. Slide onto a warm platter and cut into wedges.

Makes 4 servings

FRITTATAS

*f*rittata is the Italian word for *omelette*. Frittatas are particularly popular in the Mediterranean, where they are often served at room temperature as a tapa or snack. This flat omelette works well for 4 to 6 persons, or even a crowd, as it is easily made using many eggs and can be served at room temperature as well as hot. The filling ingredients are mixed with the eggs, or the eggs are poured over the filling in a flameproof skillet. To finish, the pan is slipped under the broiler to brown the top nicely. Some versions call for baking the frittata, then cutting it into wedges or squares to serve.

italian risotto frittata

THIS IS A FINE WAY TO UTILIZE LEFTOVER RICE, PERHAPS FROM A RISOTTO, FOR A FAST ENTRÉE FOR BRUNCH, LUNCH, OR SUPPER.

6 eggs

Salt and freshly ground pepper to taste

1 tablespoon minced fresh oregano or basil

2 tablespoons butter or olive oil

¾ cup cooked Arborio or long-grain rice

½ cup diced Fontina or Gruyère cheese

2 ounces prosciutto, cut into julienne

2 green onions, white and green parts, chopped

Cherry tomatoes and fresh basil sprigs for garnish

Preheat the broiler. In a medium bowl, beat the eggs, salt, pepper, and oregano or basil just until blended. In a 10-inch skillet, melt the butter or heat the oil over medium heat and pour in the eggs. Spoon the rice, cheese, prosciutto, and onions over the omelette and reduce heat to low. Shake the pan, slip a thin spatula under the eggs just as soon as they begin to set, and tilt the pan to let the uncooked portion flow underneath.

When the eggs are set, place under the broiler to brown the top lightly. Slide the frittata onto a warm plate and cut into wedges. Serve garnished with cherry tomatoes and basil sprigs.

Makes 3 to 4 servings

ham & sunflower seed frittata

SMOKY HAM AND SUNFLOWER SEEDS ENLIVEN BAKED CUSTARD SQUARES FOR A HIGH-PROTEIN APPETIZER.

6 eggs

¾ cup plain yogurt or low-fat sour cream

Salt and freshly ground pepper to taste

6 ounces cooked ham, finely chopped (1 cup)

2 green onions, white and green parts, chopped

2 tablespoons minced fresh flat-leaf parsley

½ cup (2 ounces) shredded Jarlsberg or Gruyère cheese

4 tablespoons hulled sunflower seeds

Preheat the oven to 350°F. Butter a 9-inch square baking pan.

In a large bowl, beat the eggs just until blended. Blend in the yogurt or sour cream, salt, pepper, ham, onions, parsley, cheese, and 2 tablespoons of the sunflower seeds. Pour into the prepared pan. Sprinkle with remaining seeds. Bake in the oven for 20 to 25 minutes, or until set. Cut into 1¾-inch squares and serve hot. (If desired, bake in advance and reheat in a 350°F oven for 10 to 15 minutes, or until heated through.)

Makes 25 squares

artichoke & red onion frittata

FRITTATAS ARE DELICIOUS AT ROOM TEMPERATURE AS WELL AS HOT. THIS ITALIAN-STYLE OMELETTE ACQUIRES A NUTTY-FLAVORED GOLDEN CRUST AS IT IS SAUTÉED IN OLIVE OIL. SERVE IT IN FAT WEDGES AS AN ENTRÉE, OR CUT INTO SMALL PORTIONS FOR AN APPETIZER.

10 ounces frozen artichoke hearts

6 eggs

Salt and freshly ground pepper to taste

3 tablespoons minced fresh flat-leaf parsley

⅓ cup (1½ ounces) grated Romano or Parmesan cheese

3 tablespoons olive oil or butter

½ cup finely chopped red onion or 3 shallots, minced

1 garlic clove, minced

2 tablespoons chopped fresh basil

Preheat the broiler. Cook the artichoke hearts in salted boiling water for 5 to 6 minutes, or until almost tender; drain. In a bowl, beat the eggs until just blended and mix in the salt, pepper, parsley, and half the cheese.

In a 10-inch skillet, heat the oil or melt the butter over medium heat and sauté the onions or shallots and garlic for 2 minutes. Add the artichoke hearts. Pour the egg mixture into the skillet, reduce the heat to low, and cook without stirring until the edges are lightly browned. Sprinkle with the remaining cheese and place under the broiler to brown the top lightly. Sprinkle with basil and cut into wedges to serve.

Makes 12 appetizers or 4 entrée servings

shrimp or crabmeat frittata

Substitute 1½ cups bay shrimp or fresh lump crabmeat for the artichoke hearts. Sauté with the shallots until just heated through. Substitute 1 tablespoon minced fresh tarragon or dill for the basil.

green onion & spinach frittata

CUT THIS VEGETABLE-STREWN BAKED OMELETTE INTO SMALL SQUARES OR DIAMONDS FOR AN APPETIZER, OR INTO LARGE RECTANGLES FOR A VEGETABLE SIDE DISH OR FIRST COURSE. THIS IS THE PARTY-SIZE VERSION; HALVE THE INGREDIENTS AND BAKE IN A 9-INCH SQUARE PAN FOR A DINNER PARTY.

2 tablespoons olive oil

4 bunches green onions, white and green parts, finely chopped

2 bunches spinach (about 2 pounds), stemmed and finely chopped

½ cup minced fresh flat-leaf parsley

¼ cup minced fresh basil

12 eggs

½ cup low-fat or regular sour cream

1½ cups (6 ounces) shredded Jarlsberg or sharp Cheddar cheese

Salt and freshly ground pepper to taste

½ cup (2 ounces) grated Parmesan cheese

Preheat the oven to 350°F. Oil a 10-by-15-inch baking pan.

In a large skillet over medium heat, heat the oil and sauté the onions until glazed. Add the spinach and sauté for 2 minutes. Remove from heat, add the parsley and basil, and set aside.

In a large bowl, beat the eggs just until blended. Blend in the sour cream, shredded cheese, salt, pepper, and onion mixture. Pour into the prepared baking pan and sprinkle with the Parmesan cheese. Bake in the oven for 25 minutes, or until set. Cut into squares and serve warm.

Makes thirty-five 2-inch appetizers or
12 side-dish or first-course servings

leek & chicken sausage frittata

SUCCULENT, SWEET LEEKS AND FLAVOR-PACKED RINGS OF CHICKEN-BASIL OR OTHER FRESH SPECIALTY SAUSAGES
FLECK THIS BAKED FRITTATA FOR A WINNING ENTRÉE OR APPETIZER. IT IS WISE TO HALVE LEEKS LENGTHWISE AND
WASH THEM THOROUGHLY TO REMOVE ANY SANDY SOIL BEFORE CHOPPING THEM.

1 tablespoon olive oil

2 large or 3 small leeks (white part only), finely chopped

6 eggs

¾ cup plain yogurt or low-fat sour cream

Salt to taste

⅛ teaspoon ground white pepper

¼ teaspoon ground nutmeg

2 tablespoons minced fresh flat-leaf parsley

¾ cup (3 ounces) shredded Jarlsberg, Gruyère, or Samsoe cheese

4 fresh chicken-basil or turkey-herb sausages, thinly sliced

Preheat the oven to 350°F. Butter a 9-inch square baking pan.

In a large skillet over medium heat, heat the oil and sauté the leeks until soft, about 7 minutes. In a large bowl, beat the eggs just until blended. Blend in the yogurt or sour cream, salt, pepper, nutmeg, parsley, cheese, leeks, and sausages. Pour into the prepared pan. Bake in the oven for 20 to 25 minutes, or until set.

Cut into 8 rectangles for an entrée or into 1¾-inch squares for appetizers. Serve hot. (If desired, bake in advance and reheat in a 350°F oven for 10 to 15 minutes, or until heated through.)

Makes 25 appetizers or 8 entrée servings

southwest frittata

THIS COLORFUL FRITTATA MAKES A HEARTY LUNCH OR SUPPER ENTRÉE. ACCOMPANY WITH MELON CRESCENTS, GRAPES, AND HOT ROLLED TORTILLAS.

4 eggs

Salt and freshly ground pepper to taste

2 teaspoons minced fresh oregano

2 tablespoons minced fresh cilantro

¼ cup sliced black or green olives

¼ cup (1 ounce) shredded Monterey jack cheese

2 tablespoons olive oil or butter

2 green onions, white and green parts, chopped

1 small red bell pepper, seeded, deribbed, and diced

6 ounces boneless, skinless chicken (breast or thigh meat), cooked and torn into strips (1 cup)

Preheat the broiler. In a bowl, beat the eggs until blended and mix in the salt, pepper, oregano, cilantro, olives, and half the cheese. In a 10-inch ovenproof skillet, heat the oil or melt the butter over medium heat and sauté the onions and pepper for 2 minutes, or until softened. Add the chicken and sauté just until heated through.

Pour the egg mixture into the skillet, reduce the heat to low, and cook without stirring until the frittata is set and the edges are lightly browned. Sprinkle with the remaining cheese. Place under the broiler to brown the top lightly. Cut into 4 wedges to serve.

Makes 4 servings

red pepper & red onion frittata

GARLICKY CROUTONS ADD CRUNCH TO THIS DECORATIVE FRITTATA FOR A GREAT-TASTING BRUNCH OR LUNCH DISH.

3 tablespoons olive oil

1 garlic clove, minced

⅓ cup sourdough bread cubes

1 red onion, diced

2 red bell peppers, seeded, deribbed, and diced

6 eggs

2 tablespoons minced fresh flat-leaf parsley

3 tablespoons minced fresh basil, plus basil sprigs for garnish

Salt and freshly ground pepper to taste

½ cup (2 ounces) shredded Fontina cheese

Preheat the oven to 350°F. Grease a 10-inch round baking dish.

In a 10-inch skillet over medium heat, heat 1 tablespoon of the oil, add the garlic and bread cubes, and shake the pan until the bread is thoroughly coated and lightly toasted, about 2 minutes; turn out of the pan. Heat the remaining 2 tablespoons oil over medium heat and sauté the onion and peppers until soft, about 5 minutes; let cool slightly.

In a medium bowl, beat the eggs just until blended and mix in the parsley, basil, salt, pepper, and sautéed vegetables. Pour into the prepared baking dish and sprinkle with the croutons and cheese. Bake in the oven for 20 minutes, or until set. Serve warm or at room temperature, garnished with basil sprigs.

Makes 4 to 6 servings

ricotta & prosciutto frittata

BLENDING RICOTTA INTO THE EGGS GIVES THIS FRITTATA A PUFFY LIFT. PROSCIUTTO AND CHARD LEND AN EMPHATIC FLAVOR NOTE.

....

2 tablespoons extra-virgin olive oil

1 small bunch red Swiss chard leaves (no stems), shredded (about 1½ cups)

1 shallot, minced

4 eggs

¼ cup ricotta cheese

1 ounce prosciutto, very thinly sliced

Salt and freshly ground pepper to taste

½ cup (2 ounces) shredded Gruyère or Emmentaler cheese

2 tablespoons minced fresh flat-leaf parsley or chives

Preheat the broiler. In a 10-inch ovenproof skillet over medium heat, heat 1 tablespoon of the oil and sauté the chard and shallot until soft, about 1 minute. In a medium bowl, beat the eggs just until blended. Mix in the ricotta, prosciutto, salt, and pepper. Mix in the chard mixture.

In the same skillet over medium heat, heat the remaining 1 tablespoon oil and pour in the eggs. Reduce the heat to low and cook, lifting from underneath, until the eggs are set. Sprinkle with the cheese and place under the broiler to brown. Serve warm or at room temperature, garnished with parsley or chives.

Makes 4 servings

tomato, basil & zucchini frittata

RESERVE THIS DECORATIVE FRITTATA FOR THE HEIGHT OF THE SUN-RIPENED TOMATO SEASON, WHEN THIS VEGETABLE IS SWEET AND BASIL IS PROLIFIC.

3 garlic cloves, minced

2 tablespoons extra-virgin olive oil

½ cup diced sourdough bread

½ cup diced red or sweet onion

2 zucchini or summer squash, sliced

4 eggs

¼ cup chopped fresh basil

Salt and freshly ground pepper to taste

2 large tomatoes, halved, seeded, and coarsely chopped

½ cup (2 ounces) shredded Asiago or dry Jack cheese

2 tablespoons minced fresh flat-leaf parsley

Preheat the oven to 350°F. In a baking dish, toss together 1 of the minced garlic cloves, 1 tablespoon of the olive oil, and the ½ cup diced sourdough bread. Bake in the oven, stirring once, for 8 to 10 minutes, or until lightly toasted. Set aside.

In a 10-inch nonstick skillet over medium heat, heat 1 teaspoon of the remaining oil and sauté the onion until soft, about 2 minutes. Add the zucchini or squash and remaining garlic and sauté for 2 minutes. Pour the vegetables into a bowl and let cool slightly.

Beat the eggs just until blended. Mix in half the basil, the salt, and pepper. Stir in the squash mixture and half of the tomatoes.

Preheat the broiler. In the same skillet over medium heat, heat the remaining 2 teaspoons oil, pour in the egg mixture, reduce the heat to low, and cook until set, lifting from the bottom. Scatter over the remaining tomatoes, the croutons, and cheese. Place the pan under the broiler until the cheese melts and the top is browned on the edges and cooked through. Sprinkle with the remaining basil and the parsley.

Makes 2 to 3 servings

mushroom medley frittata

AN EARTHY BAKED MUSHROOM FRITTATA MAKES A PERFECT AUTUMN DISH, ACCOMPANIED WITH CRISP CROSTINI OR CRUSTY COUNTRY BREADS TO DIP IN A BLEND OF OLIVE OIL AND BALSAMIC VINEGAR. CHOOSE AMONG THE VARIETY OF FRESH MUSHROOMS AVAILABLE, SUCH AS SHIITAKE, CREMINI, OYSTER MUSHROOMS, MORELS, AND PORCINI.

2 tablespoons extra-virgin olive oil or porcini oil

2 garlic cloves, minced

1 shallot, minced

12 ounces assorted mushrooms, sliced

6 eggs

1 tablespoon minced fresh tarragon or dill

Salt and freshly ground pepper to taste

½ cup (2 ounces) shredded Gruyère or Emmentaler cheese

2 tablespoons minced fresh flat-leaf parsley or chives

Preheat the oven to 350°F. Grease a 10-inch round or square baking dish.

In a large skillet over medium heat, heat the oil and sauté the garlic and shallot until soft, about 2 minutes. Add the mushrooms, increase heat to medium high, and sauté until soft, 1 to 2 minutes. Remove from heat and let cool slightly.

In a medium bowl, beat the eggs just until blended. Mix in the tarragon or dill, salt, pepper, and mushrooms. Pour into the prepared baking dish and sprinkle with the cheese. Bake in the oven for 20 minutes, or until set. Serve warm or at room temperature, garnished with parsley or chives.

Makes 4 to 6 servings

SOUFFLÉS & SOUFFLÉ OMELETTES

Soufflés combine a base of beaten egg yolks, a sauce or purée, along with beaten egg whites. The three major kinds of soufflés are savory soufflés, roulades, and dessert soufflés. A roulade is baked in a flat pan, such as a 15-by-10-inch jelly roll pan, then filled and rolled. It may be served warm or chilled.

Some soufflés can be assembled in advance, refrigerated, or even frozen and baked later. In recipes where the egg yolks are cooked with the sauce, the base becomes so sturdy that the soufflé can be baked later. This method creates a firmer soufflé than one where the egg yolks are not cooked first. I prefer not to freeze soufflés, as they must be frozen and baked in a dish that can take freezer-to-oven temperatures, such as Corning Ware, and they take twice as long to bake.

A soufflé omelette, sometimes called a puffy omelette, is a style of omelette in which the yolks and whites are beaten separately, flavorings are added, and the whole is first heated in a skillet on the stove top, then baked until browned. Though similar to a soufflé in technique, it lacks a sauce base, so it is often quicker to prepare. Unlike some soufflés, soufflé omelettes cannot be assembled in advance and baked later. They do not rise as high as a soufflé and may be baked in a regular baking dish.

SEPARATING EGGS Eggs separate more easily into yolks and whites when they are chilled. To separate eggs, crack the shell with a single brisk tap at its middle and pull the shell apart with your thumbs. Let the white run out into a small bowl, and take care not to break the yolk on the sharp edge of the shell. Put the yolk in a bowl, then transfer the white to a larger bowl. Repeat, always placing the new white in a small bowl by itself. If any trace of yolk should go in with the white, use this white for an omelette or frittata or another purpose. In this way you do not run the risk of contaminating your entire bowl of egg whites with a bit of yolk.

BEATING EGG WHITES The leavening ability of the egg depends on the amount of air beaten into it and retained during its preparation. Egg white forms a greater, more stable foam than egg yolk. When heat is applied, the air bubbles expand and the egg white stretches, then sets or coagulates, giving a light porous structure to the mixture.

Egg whites at room temperature foam more rapidly and to a greater volume than those at refrigerator temperature. Acids, such as cream of tartar, lemon juice, and vinegar (and the acid present in unlined copper bowls), stabilize the foam, since these substances cause proteins in the foam to coagulate slightly and give it strength. Sugar increases the strength of the foam and prevents overbeating, particularly with an electric beater. It also delays foaming and reduces the maximum volume. Any fat, such as an oily film on the bowl or a speck of yolk in the whites, decreases the ability of whites to foam. If your egg whites refuse to beat up properly, chances are the bowl or beater was greasy, and your only salvation is to start again with fresh egg whites and a clean bowl and beaters. Therefore, always start with a clean, dry bowl.

The bowl for beating egg whites should be stainless steel, tinned metal, or unlined copper. (If you use an unlined copper bowl, don't add cream of tartar to the whites; the acid in the copper will stabilize the whites, but can turn the whites an off color if it interacts with cream of tartar.) Porcelain and glass bowls allow the beaten whites to fall down their slippery sides and lose volume; aluminum bowls will gray the eggs; and plastic bowls, in spite of careful washing, may retain an oily film, lessening the volume. It is important that the entire mass of egg whites be in motion at once; therefore, the bowl should not be too wide and it should have a rounded bottom. Beat egg whites until stiff and glossy, not dry; at this stage the beater can be lifted and the whites will retain an upright peak. Remember that egg whites mount to seven or eight times their original volume, so choose the bowl size accordingly.

BEATING EGG YOLKS & SUGAR When beating egg yolks and sugar, beat the mixture until thick and pale in color. At this point the mixture will "form the ribbon." This means that when the mixture falls from the beater into the bowl, it will form a slowly dissolving ribbon on the surface of the mixture.

FOLDING EGG WHITES When folding egg whites into a soufflé base, first fold one-fourth of the foam into the heavy batter to lighten it. To fold, hold a rubber spatula with the blade pointing down and cut straight down through the whites in the center of the bowl. When you touch the bottom, turn the blade to scrape along the side of the bowl and lift up the batter, turning it on top of the foam. Repeat, turning the bowl a quarter turn with your other hand for each folding motion.

SOUFFLÉ DISHES The classic straight-sided soufflé dish is traditionally used for soufflés, though a round or oval copper gratin pan yields a generous surface for a crusty-topped soufflé. Individual soufflé dishes are fun and easy to serve. (Soufflé omelettes, which will not rise as high as a soufflé, are usually baked in gratin dishes or baking pans.)

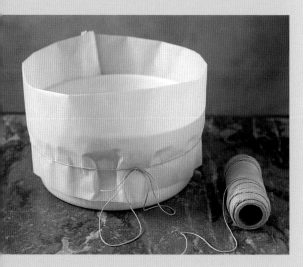

To help support a soufflé as it rises above the top of the dish, some recipes call for wrapping the dish with a collar. You can form a collar using a 12-inch-wide strip of aluminum foil or parchment paper 2 to 3 inches longer than the diameter of the dish. Fold it in half lengthwise, butter one side, and wrap the buttered side around the dish; then fold the ends twice to seal it, or secure it with paper clips or tie it with a string. Position the foil or paper so it ends about 2 inches above the top of the dish. Because the collar will deflect the heat, the soufflé will tend to sink more rapidly in the top area after baking, so my preference is to avoid a collar.

Butter the soufflé dish or baking pan amply and sprinkle bread crumbs or grated Parmesan cheese over the bottom and sides (including the collar, if using) for a savory soufflé, or granulated sugar for a dessert soufflé.

Spoon the soufflé mixture into the dish or pan, filling the dish almost to the top, so the soufflé mixture will rise up above the sides of the dish. If you want a soufflé to develop a "crown" when it puffs, draw a circle with the tip of a knife about 1 inch in from the edge of the dish and 1 inch deep. Or, slide your thumb around the rim of the mold to separate the soufflé mixture from the edge. The portion within the circle will rise higher than the mixture that surrounds it.

BAKING & SERVING SOUFFLÉS
The French bake soufflés so they are still moist and creamy in the center, providing a sauce for the crisp exterior. The soufflés in this book are all baked through until set to assure they are free of salmonella contamination. To test a soufflé for doneness, touch the center of the top; it should feel firm.

To serve soufflés, use 2 large serving spoons or salad servers. Slide one next to the dish and use the other to scoop up the soufflé.

savory SOUFFLÉS

chèvre soufflé with greens & sun-dried tomato salad

SERVE THIS CREAMY NUT-CRUSTED SOUFFLÉ FOR A DELICIOUS FIRST COURSE OR LIGHT ENTRÉE. IT IS ESPECIALLY GOOD BAKED IN A LARGE ROUND COPPER GRATIN PAN OR A 10-INCH SKILLET, YIELDING LOTS OF CRISP CRUST.

Grated Parmesan cheese for coating

4 ounces *each* cream cheese and fresh white goat cheese or 8 ounces fresh white goat cheese, at room temperature

¼ cup sour cream

4 eggs, separated

½ teaspoon salt

1 teaspoon Dijon mustard

¼ teaspoon ground nutmeg

¼ teaspoon white pepper

2 teaspoons minced fresh tarragon or ½ teaspoon dried tarragon

¼ teaspoon cream of tartar

3 tablespoons pine nuts

Preheat the oven to 425°F. Butter a 10-inch round baking dish or skillet or a 4-cup soufflé dish and sprinkle the bottom and sides with a little grated Parmesan cheese.

In a large bowl, cream the cheese until light. Beat in the sour cream, egg yolks, salt, mustard, nutmeg, pepper, and tarragon. In a large bowl, beat the egg whites until foamy. Add the cream of tartar and beat until stiff, glossy peaks form. Fold one-fourth of the beaten egg whites into the cheese mixture, then fold in the remaining egg whites. Spoon into the baking dish and smooth the top. Sprinkle with pine nuts.

Bake in the oven for 5 minutes. Reduce the temperature to 400°F and bake for 15 to 20 minutes, or until set, puffed, and golden brown.

recipe continues

chèvre soufflé with greens & sun-dried tomato salad continued

GREENS AND SUN-DRIED TOMATO SALAD

2 tablespoons red wine vinegar

1 teaspoon Dijon mustard

   Salt and freshly ground pepper
     to taste

3 tablespoons extra-virgin olive oil

1 tablespoon walnut oil

6 cups mixed salad greens

½ cup finely chopped moist-packed
   sun-dried tomatoes

Meanwhile, prepare the salad: In a small bowl, whisk the vinegar, mustard, salt, and pepper together. Whisk in the oils to emulsify. Toss the greens and tomatoes with the dressing and divide it among 6 plates. Serve a mound of soufflé alongside the salad. Serve at once.

Makes 6 servings

white cheddar soufflé with garlic croutons

GARLICKY SOURDOUGH CROUTONS SPARK THIS CHEESE-ENRICHED SOUFFLÉ. A GREEN SALAD EMBELLISHED WITH PEARS AND TOASTED HAZELNUTS OR FUJI APPLES AND WALNUTS CREATES A COMPLEMENTARY PAIRING.

1 tablespoon butter

2 slices sourdough French bread, cut into 1/2-inch cubes (1 cup)

2 garlic cloves, minced

3 eggs, separated

1 tablespoon water

3 tablespoons flour

1 cup milk

1/4 teaspoon salt

1/2 teaspoon dry mustard

1/4 teaspoon ground nutmeg

1 cup (4 ounces) shredded sharp white Cheddar cheese

1 egg white

1/4 teaspoon cream of tartar

Preheat the oven to 425°F. Butter and flour a 4-cup soufflé dish.

In a medium skillet, melt the butter over medium heat and sauté the bread cubes with the garlic until golden; set aside. In a medium bowl, whisk the egg yolks and water together. Beat in the flour until smooth. Blend in 1/4 cup of the milk. In a small saucepan, heat the remaining 3/4 cup milk to scalding and whisk it gradually into the yolk mixture. Return the mixture to the saucepan and whisk over medium heat until the mixture thickens and boils, about 1 minute. Remove from heat and stir in the salt, mustard, nutmeg, and cheese.

In a large bowl, beat the 4 egg whites until foamy. Add the cream of tartar and beat until stiff, glossy peaks form. Fold one-fourth of the beaten egg whites into the cheese sauce. Fold this mixture and the garlic croutons into the remaining egg whites. Spoon into the prepared dish and bake in the oven for 5 minutes. Reduce the temperature to 400°F and bake for 15 to 20 minutes, or until set and golden brown. Serve immediately.

Makes 2 to 4 servings

note: This soufflé can be assembled, refrigerated, and baked later. If chilled, increase the baking time by 5 to 10 minutes.

soufflé omelette bon laboureur

A FRENCH COUNTRY INN LOCATED AT CHENONCEAUX IN THE LOIRE VALLEY MAKES A SPECIALTY OF THIS HERB-SCENTED SOUFFLÉ OMELETTE. IT RESEMBLES A BALLOON-SIZED BLIMP AS IT ARRIVES ON THE DINER'S TABLE. THE CHEF BROWNS THE SOUFFLÉ IN A SKILLET AND THEN TRANSFERS IT TO A BAKING PLATTER FOR FINAL BAKING TO ACHIEVE A ROUNDED LOOK.

6 eggs, separated

½ teaspoon salt

½ teaspoon cream of tartar

1 teaspoon minced fresh flat-leaf parsley

1 teaspoon minced chives

1 teaspoon minced tarragon

2 tablespoons unsalted butter

Preheat the oven to 375°F. In a large bowl, beat the egg whites until foamy. Add the salt and cream of tartar and beat until stiff, glossy peaks form. In a medium bowl, beat the yolks until thick and pale in color. Stir in the herbs. Fold one-fourth of the beaten egg whites into the yolk mixture. Fold this mixture into the remaining egg whites.

In a flameproof 6-cup oval baking dish or 10-inch skillet, melt the butter over medium heat and spoon in the soufflé, mounding it higher in the center. Cook until set on the bottom, about 3 minutes. Bake in the oven for 10 minutes, or until set through and golden. Serve at once.

Makes 4 to 6 servings

spinach soufflé

THIS BASIC VEGETABLE SOUFFLÉ CAN BE VARIED WITH MANY FLAVOR COMBINATIONS.

¾ cup (3 ounces) shredded
    Gruyère or Jarlsberg cheese

1 cup milk

3 tablespoons cornstarch mixed
    with 3 tablespoons water

¾ teaspoon salt

¼ teaspoon ground nutmeg

2 teaspoons butter

1 small onion, finely chopped

1 large bunch spinach (1 pound),
    stemmed and finely chopped

6 eggs, separated

¼ teaspoon cream of tartar

Preheat the oven to 375°F. Butter an 8-cup soufflé dish and sprinkle the bottom and sides with 2 tablespoons of the shredded cheese.

In a medium saucepan, heat the milk until scalded; add the cornstarch mixture and stir over medium heat until thickened. Stir in the salt and nutmeg and set aside.

In a large skillet, melt the butter over medium heat and cook the onion until softened, about 5 minutes. Add the spinach and cook just until heated through and still slightly crisp, about 1 minute; drain off any liquid. In a blender or food processor, purée the spinach and egg yolks until the spinach is minced. Stir the spinach mixture into the cornstarch-thickened sauce. Mix in the remaining cheese.

In a large bowl, beat the egg whites until foamy. Add the cream of tartar and beat until stiff, glossy peaks form. Fold one-fourth of the beaten egg whites into the spinach mixture. Fold this mixture into the remaining egg whites. Spoon the batter into the prepared soufflé dish; smooth the surface. Bake in the oven for 35 minutes, or until puffed and golden brown.

Makes 6 to 8 servings

recipe continues

broccoli soufflé

Substitute 1½ cups chopped cooked broccoli florets for the spinach. Purée the broccoli-onion mixture and egg yolks until the broccoli is minced. Proceed as directed above.

mushroom soufflé

Substitute 1⅓ cups (about 6 ounces) chopped cultivated brown mushrooms for the spinach, sautéing them with the onion and ½ teaspoon dried tarragon until glazed. Purée the mushroom-onion mixture with the egg yolks until the mushrooms are minced. Proceed as directed above.

asparagus soufflé

Substitute 1½ cups diced cooked asparagus tips for the spinach. Purée the asparagus-onion mixture and egg yolks until the asparagus is minced. Proceed as directed above.

southern spoon bread soufflé

THIS SOUFFLÉ-LIKE HOT BREAD IS A FAVORITE SOUTHERN ACCOMPANIMENT TO HAM, ROAST PORK, OR BARBECUED CHICKEN. FOR A SOUTHWEST VARIATION, ADD CORN AND CHILIES.

1¼ cups milk

¾ cup yellow cornmeal

2 tablespoons sugar

½ teaspoon salt

Dash of hot pepper sauce

3 tablespoons butter

4 eggs, separated

¼ teaspoon cream of tartar

Preheat the oven to 375°F. Butter a 4-cup soufflé dish.

In a medium saucepan, heat the milk just to boiling and gradually stir in the cornmeal. Reduce the heat to low and cook, stirring occasionally, until the cornmeal is thickened, about 10 minutes. Stir in the sugar, salt, hot sauce, and butter and remove from heat.

In a large bowl, beat the egg yolks until thick and pale in color. Stir in the hot cornmeal mixture. In a large bowl, beat the egg whites until foamy. Add the cream of tartar and beat until stiff, glossy peaks form. Fold one-fourth of the beaten egg whites into the cornmeal mixture. Fold this mixture into the remaining egg whites. Turn into the prepared dish and bake in the oven for 35 minutes, or until set and golden brown.

Makes 6 servings

southwest variation

Into the hot cornmeal mixture, stir 1 cup fresh white or yellow corn kernels and 3 tablespoons sautéed minced fresh green chilies, such as jalapeños for a hot flavor, or Anaheims for a milder flavor. Or use canned chilies. Fold in the beaten egg whites and bake as directed above.

salmon soufflé roulade

PINWHEELS OF A SAVORY SOUFFLÉ WITH A SMOKED SALMON AND SOUR-CREAM FILLING ARE A STELLAR FIRST COURSE OR LUNCHEON ENTRÉE. MAKE IN ADVANCE EARLY IN THE DAY AND REFRIGERATE IF YOU WISH TO SERVE COLD.

SOUFFLÉ SHEET

4 tablespoons butter

⅓ cup all-purpose flour

1¼ cups milk, heated

½ teaspoon salt

1 tablespoon brandy or sherry

¼ teaspoon ground nutmeg

5 eggs, separated

¼ cup (1 ounce) grated Parmesan cheese

¼ teaspoon cream of tartar

SALMON FILLING

1 cup (8 ounces) sour cream

6 ounces smoked salmon, diced

1 teaspoon grated lemon zest

2 tablespoons capers, drained

2 green onions, white and green parts, finely chopped

Cherry tomatoes for garnish

To make the soufflé sheet: Preheat the oven to 375°F. Line a 10-by-15-inch baking pan with parchment paper or waxed paper. Heavily butter and flour the paper.

In a medium saucepan, melt the butter over medium heat and blend in the flour; cook and stir for 2 minutes. Gradually whisk in the milk, blending with a wire whisk, and cook, stirring, until thickened. Remove from heat and stir in the salt, brandy or sherry, nutmeg, and egg yolks, one at a time. Mix in the cheese.

In a large bowl, beat the egg whites until foamy. Add the cream of tartar and beat until stiff, glossy peaks form. Fold one-fourth of the beaten egg whites into the yolk mixture. Fold this mixture into the remaining egg whites. Spread the batter evenly in the prepared pan.

Bake in the oven for 15 minutes, or until the soufflé is golden brown and the top springs back when touched lightly. Turn the pan upside down on a cloth towel. Remove the pan and peel off the paper.

recipe continues

To make the filling: Mix all the filling ingredients together and spread over the soufflé. Roll up jelly-roll fashion from a lengthwise side. Place on a serving platter and garnish with cherry tomatoes. Serve warm or chilled, cut into 1-inch-thick slices.

Makes 6 to 8 servings

spinach soufflé roll with seafood

A SMOKED TROUT OR SALMON FILLING SPIRALS INSIDE THIS SAVORY SPINACH LOG FOR A SUMPTUOUS ENTRÉE OR FIRST COURSE. SERVE WITH A GREEN SALAD WITH CHERRY TOMATOES AND MUSHROOMS, AND A CRUSTY COUNTRY-STYLE BREAD.

2 tablespoons extra-virgin olive oil

2 bunches spinach, stemmed and chopped

2 green onions, white and green parts, chopped

5 eggs, separated

¼ teaspoon salt

¼ teaspoon cream of tartar

Dash of ground white pepper to taste

¼ teaspoon ground nutmeg

1 cup (8 ounces) sour cream

¾ cup (3 ounces) grated Parmesan or Romano cheese

6 ounces flaked smoked trout or cooked salmon, or cooked bay shrimp (1 cup)

1 shallot, minced

3 tablespoons minced fresh flat-leaf parsley

Preheat the oven to 375°F. Line a 10-by-15-inch baking pan with parchment paper or waxed paper; heavily butter and flour the paper.

In a large skillet over medium heat, heat the oil and cook the spinach and onions until slightly wilted, about 2 minutes. Drain off any liquid and purée the vegetables in a blender or food processor.

In a large bowl, beat the egg whites until foamy. Add the salt and cream of tartar and beat until stiff, glossy peaks form. In a large bowl, beat the egg yolks until thick and pale in color. Mix in the pepper, nutmeg, ⅓ cup of the sour cream, ½ cup of the cheese, and the spinach mixture. Fold one-fourth of the beaten egg whites into the egg yolk mixture. Fold this mixture into the remaining egg whites. Turn into the prepared pan and sprinkle with the remaining cheese.

Bake in the oven for 15 to 20 minutes, or until the top springs back when lightly touched. Invert immediately on a cloth towel, remove the pan, and peel off the paper. Let cool 5 minutes.

recipe continues

In a small bowl, combine the remaining ⅔ cup sour cream, the seafood, shallot, and parsley. Spread the sour cream mixture over the soufflé sheet. Roll the sheet up jelly-roll fashion from one long side and place on a platter. Serve hot, at room temperature, or chilled, cut into 1-inch-thick slices.

Makes 8 servings

glazed apple soufflé omelette

CARAMELIZED APPLE SLICES SPICE THIS CALVADOS-SCENTED SOUFFLÉ.

2 tablespoons butter

8 tablespoons sugar

½ teaspoon ground cinnamon

3 Granny Smith or Golden
  Delicious apples, peeled,
  cored, and sliced

4 eggs, separated

⅛ teaspoon salt

¼ teaspoon cream of tartar

1 tablespoon Calvados or brandy

Whipped cream flavored with
  Calvados or frozen yogurt
  for serving

Preheat the oven to 375°F. In a large ovenproof skillet, melt the butter with 2 tablespoons of the sugar and the cinnamon over medium heat and sauté the apple slices until soft, turning them frequently.

In a large bowl, beat the egg whites until foamy. Add the salt and cream of tartar and beat until soft peaks form. Beat in 2 tablespoons of the sugar until stiff, glossy peaks form. In a medium bowl, beat the egg yolks until thick and pale in color. Beat in the remaining 4 tablespoons sugar and the Calvados or brandy. Fold in the beaten egg whites and spoon over the glazed apples.

Bake in the oven for 15 minutes, or until golden brown and set. Serve at once, with whipped cream or frozen yogurt.

Makes 4 servings

chocolate-almond soufflé omelette

CHOCOLATE STREAKS THIS SOUFFLÉ, AND CARAMELIZED ALMONDS GILD THE UNDERSIDE FOR A SUMPTUOUS SWEET.

1 tablespoon butter

6 tablespoons sugar

¼ cup finely chopped blanched
almonds or skinned hazelnuts

4 eggs, separated

⅛ teaspoon salt

¼ teaspoon cream of tartar

2 tablespoons amaretto or rum

2 ounces bittersweet chocolate,
finely chopped (⅓ cup)

Whipped cream, frozen vanilla
yogurt, or ice cream for serving

Preheat the oven to 375°F. In a 10-inch ovenproof skillet, melt the butter and 1 tablespoon of the sugar over medium heat. Add the nuts and sauté until lightly toasted. Remove from heat.

In a large bowl, beat the egg whites until foamy. Add the salt and cream of tartar and beat until soft peaks form. Beat in 2 tablespoons of the sugar until stiff, glossy peaks form. In a medium bowl, beat the egg yolks until thick and pale in color. Beat in the remaining 3 tablespoons sugar and amaretto or rum. Fold in the beaten egg whites and chocolate. Spoon into the nut-crusted skillet.

Bake in the oven for 15 minutes, or until golden brown and set. Serve at once, with whipped cream, frozen yogurt, or ice cream.

Makes 4 servings

rum soufflé omelette with plum sauce

THIS PUFFY OMELETTE IS LOVELY WITH A FRUIT ACCOMPANIMENT. IN SEASON, SERVE WITH THE PLUM SAUCE; AT ANOTHER TIME OFFER SLICED MANGOES, PEACHES, OR NECTARINES.

PLUM SAUCE

12 ounces plums, pitted and sliced (1½ cups)

2 tablespoons honey

½ teaspoon ground cinnamon

2 tablespoons orange juice or cranberry juice

4 eggs, separated

⅛ teaspoon salt

¼ teaspoon cream of tartar

6 tablespoons sugar

2 tablespoons rum

2 teaspoons grated lemon zest

1 tablespoon flour

Powdered sugar for dusting

To make the sauce: In a medium saucepan, combine all the sauce ingredients. Bring to a boil, reduce heat, and simmer, uncovered, for 10 minutes, or until soft. Let cool. If desired, make in advance.

Preheat the oven to 375°F. Generously butter a 10-inch round or oval baking dish or ovenproof skillet.

In a large bowl, beat the egg whites until foamy. Add the salt and cream of tartar and beat until soft peaks form. Gradually add the sugar, beating until stiff, glossy peaks form. In a medium bowl, beat the egg yolks until thick and pale in color. Beat in the rum, lemon zest, and flour. Fold in the beaten egg whites. Spoon into the prepared dish and dust with powdered sugar.

Bake in the oven for 15 minutes, or until golden brown and set. Serve warm, with plum sauce or fresh fruit.

Makes 4 servings

salzburger nockerls

IN THE PICTURESQUE OLD TOWN OF SALZBURG, AUSTRIA, THE RENOWNED GOLDENER HIRSCH MAKES A SPECIALTY OF THIS FAMOUS DISH. ON A TRIP I TOOK WITH AMERICAN FOOD EDITORS, THE CHEF GAVE US A DEMONSTRATION AND SHARED THE FORMULA FOR THIS SWEET DUMPLING. THE ORIGINAL RECIPE IS SAID TO BE A COUPLE HUNDRED YEARS OLD. IN A DELICIOUS EXCEPTION TO TRADITION, PRESERVES AND CHOCOLATE CURLS HERE LEND EMBELLISHMENT.

2 tablespoons unsalted butter

¼ cup apricot preserves or orange marmalade

6 eggs, separated

2 egg whites

⅛ teaspoon salt

¼ teaspoon cream of tartar

6 tablespoons sugar

2 tablespoons flour

1 teaspoon grated lemon zest

Powdered sugar for dusting

1 ounce bittersweet chocolate, cut into curls, for garnish

Whipped cream, sweetened and flavored with vanilla, for serving (optional)

Preheat the oven to 375°F. In a 10-inch baking pan or oven-proof skillet, melt the butter with the preserves over medium heat.

In a large bowl, beat the 8 egg whites until foamy. Add the salt and cream of tartar and beat until soft peaks form. Gradually add the sugar, beating until stiff, glossy peaks form. In a medium bowl, beat the egg yolks until thick and pale in color. Beat in the flour and lemon zest to blend thoroughly. Fold one-fourth of the whites into the yolks, then fold in the remainder. Spoon into 4 rounded ovals in the baking dish. Dust with powdered sugar.

Bake in the oven for 15 to 20 minutes, or until the tops are lightly browned. Serve at once, with chocolate curls sprinkled over each serving, and whipped cream, if desired.

Makes 4 servings

orange soufflé omelette

ORANGE ZEST AND ORANGE JUICE CONCENTRATE ARE THE SECRETS TO THE ZINGY FLAVOR OF THIS QUICK
OMELETTE THAT IS IDEAL FOR BRUNCH OR DESSERT.

4 eggs, separated

⅛ teaspoon salt

¼ teaspoon cream of tartar

6 tablespoons sugar

3 tablespoons orange juice
  concentrate, thawed

2 teaspoons grated orange zest

1 tablespoon flour

1 tablespoon Triple Sec, Grand
  Marnier, or other orange-
  flavored liqueur

Powdered sugar for dusting

Orange slices or sections, or
  halved and sugared fresh
  strawberries

Preheat the oven to 375°F. Generously butter a 10-inch round
or oval baking dish or ovenproof skillet.

In a large bowl, beat the egg whites until foamy. Add the salt
and cream of tartar and beat until soft peaks form. Gradually
add the sugar, beating until stiff, glossy peaks form. In a
medium bowl, beat the egg yolks until thick and pale in color.
Beat in the orange juice concentrate, zest, flour, and liqueur.
Fold in the beaten egg whites. Spoon into the prepared dish
or pan. Dust with powdered sugar.

Bake in the oven for 15 minutes, or until golden brown and
set. Serve warm, with fruit.

Makes 4 servings

lemon custard soufflé with raspberries

THAT DECADES-OLD FAVORITE, LEMON PUDDING WITH A SOUFFLÉ CROWN, GETS A TANGY-SWEET UPDATE WITH A
LAYER OF RASPBERRIES UNDERNEATH.

1 cup fresh raspberries

2 tablespoons butter at room
  temperature

¾ cup sugar

2 teaspoons grated lemon zest

3 eggs, separated

3 tablespoons flour

⅓ cup fresh lemon juice

1 cup milk

⅛ teaspoon salt

¼ teaspoon cream of tartar

Powdered sugar for dusting

Preheat the oven to 350°F. Spoon the raspberries into the bottom of a 6-cup soufflé dish or four 8-ounce soufflé dishes.

In a medium bowl, cream the butter, ½ cup of the sugar, and the lemon zest together until fluffy. Beat in the egg yolks, flour, lemon juice, and milk. In a large bowl, beat the egg whites until foamy. Add the salt and cream of tartar and beat until soft peaks form. Gradually add the remaining ¼ cup sugar, beating until stiff, glossy peaks form. Fold into the yolk mixture and spoon the batter over the raspberries. Place the dish in a baking pan filled with 1 inch of hot water.

Bake in the oven for 30 minutes, or until set. Dust with powdered sugar and serve warm or at room temperature.

Makes 4 servings

dark-chocolate soufflé

THIS DELECTABLE SOUFFLÉ IS PARTICULARLY EASY TO ASSEMBLE, AND IT CAN BE MADE AS MANY AS 24 HOURS IN ADVANCE AND BAKED JUST BEFORE SERVING.

7 eggs, separated

⅛ teaspoon salt

½ teaspoon cream of tartar

¾ cup sugar

1 teaspoon vanilla extract, or
1 tablespoon Cointreau or
framboise liqueur

6 ounces bittersweet or semisweet
chocolate, chopped, melted,
and cooled

Whipped cream, sweetened to
taste, or vanilla ice cream or
frozen yogurt for serving

Butter a 6-cup soufflé dish, a 10-inch round baking dish, or 8 individual soufflé dishes, about 8 ounces each. Dust the bottom and sides of the dishes with sugar.

In a large bowl, beat the egg whites until foamy. Add the salt and cream of tartar and beat until soft peaks form. Gradually add ¼ cup of the sugar, beating until stiff, glossy peaks form. In a medium bowl, beat the yolks until thick and pale in color. Beat in the remaining ½ cup sugar and the vanilla or liqueur. Stir in the melted chocolate. Fold one-fourth of the beaten egg whites into the chocolate mixture. Fold this mixture into the remaining whites.

Spoon the soufflé mixture into the prepared dishes. If making in advance, cover with plastic wrap and let sit at room temperature for up to 1 hour, or refrigerate for up to 24 hours.

Preheat the oven to 375°F for the large soufflé or 400°F for individual soufflés. Bake the large soufflé in the oven for 30 to 35 minutes or the individual soufflés for 10 to 12 minutes, or until set. Add a few minutes to the baking time if refrigerated. Serve with whipped cream, ice cream, or frozen yogurt.

Makes 8 servings

surprise omelette with berries

THE ORIGIN OF THIS CONFECTION IS CREDITED TO A CHINESE CHEF WHO VISITED PARIS IN THE 1860S. HE DELIGHTED GUESTS AT THE GRAND HOTEL WITH HIS GINGER AND VANILLA ICES ENVELOPED IN HOT MERINGUE. THIS RECIPE IS BASED ON A MASTERPIECE I SAMPLED IN PARIS, FEATURING STRAWBERRY SORBET AND HAZELNUT AND PRALINE ICE CREAMS ENCASED IN A CLOUD OF SOUFFLÉ AND FLAMED AT TABLESIDE WITH KIRSCH.

1 pint toasted almond ice cream, slightly softened

1 pint strawberry sorbet, slightly softened

One 8-inch sponge cake layer, homemade or purchased

2 tablespoons kirsch

4 egg whites

⅛ teaspoon salt

¼ teaspoon cream of tartar

½ cup sugar

2 egg yolks

1 teaspoon vanilla extract

Powdered sugar for dusting

2 cups fresh strawberries, hulled, sliced, and sugared

In a round-bottomed bowl about 8 inches in diameter, pack the ice cream and sorbet in 2 layers; cover and freeze until firm, about 2 hours. Place the cake layer on an ovenproof platter and drizzle with kirsch. Unmold the ice cream by dipping the bowl in a bowl of hot water for 5 seconds. Invert on the cake. Place in the freezer while preparing the soufflé.

Preheat the oven to 500°F. In a large bowl, beat the egg whites until foamy. Add the salt and cream of tartar and beat until soft peaks form. Gradually add the sugar, beating until stiff, glossy peaks form. In a medium bowl, beat the egg yolks until thick and pale in color. Beat in the vanilla. Fold in the beaten egg whites. Spoon the soufflé over the top and sides of the ice cream–covered cake, covering it completely. Dust lightly with powdered sugar.

Bake in the oven for 3 to 4 minutes, or until golden brown. Serve at once, cut into wedges, and accompanied with berries.

Makes 6 to 8 servings

swedish sour cream soufflé omelette with berries

THIS EASY-TO-ASSEMBLE CREAMY SOUFFLÉ IS ELEGANT ACCOMPANIED WITH RASPBERRIES OR A MIXED-BERRY MEDLEY OF RASPBERRIES, STRAWBERRIES, AND BLUEBERRIES, AND TOPPED WITH WHIPPED CREAM SCENTED WITH FRAMBOISE.

6 eggs, separated

⅛ teaspoon salt

¼ teaspoon cream of tartar

8 tablespoons sugar

6 tablespoons sour cream

1 teaspoon grated lemon zest

FRAMBOISE WHIPPED CREAM

¾ cup heavy (whipping) cream

2 teaspoons powdered sugar

2 teaspoons framboise liqueur or
   ½ teaspoon vanilla extract

1½ cups fresh raspberries or
   mixed fresh raspberries,
   halved strawberries, and
   blueberries, lightly sugared,
   for serving

Preheat the oven to 375°F. Butter a 10-inch round or oval baking dish.

In a large bowl, beat the egg whites until foamy. Add the salt and cream of tartar and beat until soft peaks form. Gradually add 2 tablespoons of the sugar, beating until stiff, glossy peaks form. In a medium bowl, beat the egg yolks until thick and pale in color. Beat in the remaining 6 tablespoons sugar. Mix in the sour cream and lemon zest. Fold in the beaten egg whites. Spoon into the prepared dish. Bake in the oven for 15 minutes, or until golden brown and set.

Meanwhile, make the whipped cream: In a deep bowl, beat the cream until soft peaks form. Beat in the powdered sugar and framboise or vanilla. Serve the soufflé at once, accompanied with a bowl of whipped cream and the berries.

Makes 6 servings

white chocolate soufflé with raspberry sauce

A RUBY BERRY SAUCE GILDS THIS SNOWY WHITE SOUFFLÉ FOR AN EYE-CATCHING FINISH.

3 ounces white chocolate, chopped

4 eggs, separated

⅛ teaspoon salt

¼ teaspoon cream of tartar

6 tablespoons sugar

1 teaspoon vanilla extract or
  1 tablespoon framboise liqueur

RASPBERRY SAUCE

1 cup fresh or frozen unsweetened
  raspberries, thawed

Sugar to taste

Preheat the oven to 400°F. Butter 4 individual soufflé dishes, about 8 ounces each. Lightly dust the bottom and sides of the dishes with sugar. Melt the chocolate over barely simmering water; set aside to cool.

In a large bowl, beat the egg whites until foamy. Add the salt and cream of tartar, and beat until soft peaks form. Gradually add 2 tablespoons of the sugar, beating until stiff, glossy peaks form. In a medium bowl, beat the egg yolks until thick and pale in color. Beat in the remaining 4 tablespoons sugar. Stir in the vanilla or framboise and the melted chocolate. Fold one-fourth of the beaten egg whites into the chocolate mixture. Fold this mixture into the remaining egg whites. Spoon the soufflé mixture into the prepared dishes. Bake for 10 minutes, or until set and golden brown.

Meanwhile, make the sauce: Purée the raspberries in a blender and push them through a sieve, discarding the seeds. Sweeten to taste. Pour the sauce into a pitcher. Slash each soufflé with a spoon and pour in a little sauce.

Makes 4 servings

pooh's honey soufflé

THIS HONEY-SCENTED SOUFFLÉ IS LOVELY SERVED WITH WHIPPED CREAM, LONG CURLS OF CHOCOLATE, AND A FEW TANGY RASPBERRIES OR BLUEBERRIES.

6 eggs, separated

⅛ teaspoon salt

¼ teaspoon cream of tartar

2 tablespoons sugar

⅔ cup orange-flower or other mild honey

2 teaspoons grated lemon zest

2 tablespoons flour

2 tablespoons butter, melted

Whipped cream, sweetened to taste, for serving

1 cup sugared fresh raspberries or blueberries for serving

Chocolate curls for garnish (optional)

Preheat the oven to 375°F. Butter a 6-cup soufflé dish. Clip or tie on an aluminum-foil collar around the top of the dish (see page 45). Lightly dust the bottom and sides of the dish and the collar with sugar.

In a large bowl, beat the egg whites until foamy. Add the salt and cream of tartar and beat until soft peaks form. Gradually add the sugar, beating until stiff, glossy peaks form. In a medium bowl, beat the egg yolks until thick and pale in color. Beat in the honey, lemon zest, flour, and butter. Fold one-fourth of the beaten egg whites into the egg yolk mixture. Fold this mixture into the remaining egg whites. Spoon into the soufflé dish.

Bake in the oven for 30 to 35 minutes, or until golden brown and set. Serve at once with whipped cream, berries, and chocolate curls, if desired.

Makes 6 servings

grand marnier soufflé

THIS DELECTABLE SOUFFLÉ ALWAYS BRINGS ACCOLADES. LET IT STAR AT A SIMPLE SOUP OR SALAD SUPPER. IT MAKES A LOVELY FINALE TO GRILLED SALMON OR TIGER PRAWNS.

¾ cup milk

2 tablespoons cornstarch

8 tablespoons sugar

2 tablespoons butter

⅓ cup Grand Marnier

2 teaspoons grated orange zest

4 eggs, separated

2 egg whites

⅛ teaspoon salt

¼ teaspoon cream of tartar

1 cup heavy cream, whipped and sweetened, or custard sauce for serving

Preheat the oven to 375°F. Butter a 6-cup soufflé dish or baking dish and dust the bottom and sides lightly with sugar.

In a small saucepan, blend ¼ cup of the milk with the cornstarch. Stir in the remaining ½ cup milk and 6 tablespoons of the sugar and cook, stirring, over medium heat until thickened. Blend in the butter, Grand Marnier, and orange zest. Whisk in the egg yolks, one at a time.

In a large bowl, beat the 6 egg whites until foamy. Add the salt and cream of tartar and beat until soft peaks form. Beat in the remaining 2 tablespoons sugar and beat until stiff, glossy peaks form. Fold one-fourth of the beaten egg whites into the egg yolk mixture. Fold this mixture into the remaining egg whites. Spoon into the prepared dish.

Bake in the oven for 30 to 35 minutes, or until set and golden brown. Serve at once, with whipped cream or custard sauce.

Makes 6 to 8 servings

coconut soufflé with mangoes & kiwifruit

AS THE FINISHING TOUCH FOR A MENU WITH TROPICAL OVERTONES, THIS SOUFFLÉ IS SUBLIME. OFFER A PLATTER OF SLICED MANGO AND KIWIFRUIT FOR A COMPLEMENTARY PARTNER.

3 tablespoons butter

¼ cup all-purpose flour

1 cup milk, heated

4 eggs, separated

6 tablespoons sugar

1 cup shredded sweetened coconut

½ teaspoon almond extract

2 teaspoons vanilla extract

2 egg whites

⅛ teaspoon salt

¼ teaspoon cream of tartar

Sliced mango and kiwifruit for serving

Almond Ice Cream Sauce (recipe follows), optional

Preheat the oven to 375°F. Butter a 6-cup oval gratin dish or soufflé dish and dust the bottom and sides with sugar.

In a medium saucepan, melt the butter over medium heat and blend in the flour; cook, stirring, for 2 minutes. Gradually stir in the milk and cook, stirring constantly, until thickened. In a medium bowl, beat the egg yolks until thick and pale in color and beat in 2 tablespoons of the sugar. Gradually stir the sauce into the egg yolk mixture; mix in the coconut and almond and vanilla extracts; set aside.

In a large bowl, beat the 6 egg whites until foamy. Add the salt and cream of tartar and beat until soft peaks form. Gradually add the remaining 4 tablespoons sugar, beating until stiff, glossy peaks form. Fold one-fourth of the beaten egg whites into the coconut mixture. Fold this mixture into the remaining egg whites. Turn into the prepared dish.

Bake in the oven for 35 minutes, or until set and golden brown. Serve immediately, with fruit and Almond Ice Cream Sauce, if desired.

Makes 6 servings

recipe continues

almond ice cream sauce

In a deep bowl, beat ½ cup heavy (whipping) cream until stiff peaks form. Beat in 1 tablespoon amaretto or ½ teaspoon almond extract and 1½ pints softened toasted almond ice cream just until smooth and fluffy. Turn into a freezer container and freeze until barely set, about 1 hour.

hazelnut praline soufflé

A TOUCH OF RUM PERVADES THIS CRUNCHY NUT SOUFFLÉ, LENDING AN AROMATIC PIZZAZZ.

4 tablespoons butter

¼ cup flour

1 cup milk

⅔ cup sugar

6 eggs, separated

¼ cup dark rum or amaretto

⅛ teaspoon salt

¼ teaspoon cream of tartar

Praline (recipe follows)

Whipped cream or frozen vanilla or coffee yogurt for serving

Butter a 6-cup soufflé dish. Clip or tie an aluminum-foil collar around the top of the dish (see page 45). Dust the bottom and sides of the dish and the collar lightly with sugar. Preheat the oven to 375°F.

In a medium saucepan, melt the butter over medium heat and blend in the flour; cook, stirring, for 2 minutes. Gradually stir in the milk and ⅓ cup of the sugar. Cook, stirring, until the sauce comes to a boil, and boil for 30 seconds. Remove from heat and whisk in the egg yolks, one at a time. Stir in the rum or amaretto.

In a large bowl, beat the egg whites until foamy. Add the salt and cream of tartar and beat until soft peaks form. Gradually add the remaining ⅓ cup sugar, beating until stiff, glossy peaks form. Fold one-fourth of the beaten egg whites and all the praline into the egg yolk mixture. Fold this mixture into the remaining egg whites. Spoon into prepared soufflé dish.

Bake in the oven for 35 minutes, or until set. Serve at once, with whipped cream or frozen yogurt.

Makes 6 to 8 servings

recipe continues

praline

In a small, heavy skillet over medium-high heat, heat 6 table-spoons sugar until it melts and turns amber. Add 6 table-spoons chopped skinned hazelnuts or blanched almonds and shake to coat the nuts with caramel. Turn out onto buttered aluminum foil; let cool and chop finely.

ricotta-rum soufflé with peaches

THIS ETHEREAL CHEESE SOUFFLÉ IS DELIGHTFUL SERVED WARM FROM THE OVEN WITH SLICED PEACHES OR SUGARED BOYSENBERRIES. ONCE IT DEFLATES, IT IS EXCELLENT CHILLED AS WELL.

1½ cups (12 ounces) ricotta cheese

6 ounces light cream cheese or goat cheese at room temperature

4 eggs, separated

3 tablespoons flour

1 cup plus 2 tablespoons sugar

2 teaspoons grated lemon zest

¼ cup dark rum

⅛ teaspoon salt

¼ teaspoon cream of tartar

Powdered sugar for dusting

Fresh sliced peaches or sugared berries for serving

Preheat the oven to 350°F. Butter and flour a 9-inch springform pan.

In a large bowl, cream the cheeses until light. Beat in the egg yolks. Stir the flour and the 1 cup sugar together. Stir the flour mixture into the cheese mixture with the lemon zest and rum.

In a large bowl, beat the egg whites until foamy. Add the salt and cream of tartar and beat until soft peaks form. Gradually add the 2 tablespoons sugar, beating until stiff, glossy peaks form. Fold one-fourth of the beaten egg whites into the cheese mixture. Fold this mixture into the remaining egg whites. Turn into the prepared pan.

Bake in the oven for 30 to 35 minutes, or until set and golden brown. Serve warm, dusted with powdered sugar and accompanied with fruit. Or, let cool and serve chilled.

Makes 6 to 8 servings

apricot soufflé

THIS IS WONDERFULLY EASY TO ASSEMBLE AND CREATES A BEAUTIFUL HOT OR COLD DESSERT THAT HOLDS ITS SHAPE WELL AFTER BAKING. IF YOU CHOOSE TO OMIT THE WHIPPED CREAM FOR A FAT-FREE CONFECTION, EMBELLISH EACH SERVING WITH A NASTURTIUM BLOSSOM OR A FEW STRAWBERRIES.

3/4 cup (4 ounces) dried apricots

1 cup water

1/4 teaspoon almond extract

4 egg whites

1/8 teaspoon salt

1/4 teaspoon cream of tartar

3 tablespoons sugar

FLAVORED WHIPPED CREAM

3/4 cup heavy (whipping) cream

Sugar to taste

1 tablespoon brandy or amaretto (optional)

Preheat the oven to 425°F. Butter a 4-cup soufflé dish and dust it lightly with sugar.

In a small saucepan, cook the apricots in the water just until tender, about 10 minutes. Let cool. In a blender, purée the apricots and liquid with the almond extract. (You should have 1 cup very thick purée.)

In a large bowl, beat the egg whites until foamy. Add the salt and cream of tartar and beat until soft peaks form. Gradually add the sugar, beating until stiff, glossy peaks form. Fold one-fourth of the beaten egg whites into the apricot mixture. Fold this mixture into the remaining egg whites. Turn into the prepared dish.

Bake in the oven for 10 minutes, or until set. Watch carefully, as it browns quickly on top.

Meanwhile, to make the flavored whipped cream: In a deep bowl, beat the cream until soft peaks form. Fold in the sugar and the brandy or amaretto, if desired. Serve the soufflé at once, with the whipped cream, or serve cold.

Makes 6 servings

INDEX

TABLE OF EQUIVALENTS

The exact equivalents in the following tables have been rounded for convenience.

LIQUID AND DRY MEASURES

U.S.	Metric
¼ teaspoon	1.25 milliliters
½ teaspoon	2.5 milliliters
1 teaspoon	5 milliliters
1 tablespoon (3 teaspoons)	15 milliliters
1 fluid ounce (2 tablespoons)	30 milliliters
¼ cup	60 milliliters
⅓ cup	80 milliliters
½ cup	120 milliliters
1 cup	240 milliliters
1 pint (2 cups)	480 milliliters
1 quart (4 cups, 32 ounces)	960 milliliters
1 gallon (4 quarts)	3.84 liters
1 ounce (by weight)	28 grams
1 pound	454 grams
2.2 pounds	1 kilogram

LENGTH MEASURES

U.S.	Metric
⅛ inch	3 millimeters
¼ inch	6 millimeters
½ inch	12 millimeters
1 inch	2.5 centimeters

OVEN TEMPERATURES

Fahrenheit	Celsius	Gas
250	120	½
275	140	1
300	150	2
325	160	3
350	180	4
375	190	5
400	200	6
425	220	7
450	230	8
475	240	9
500	260	10